She:

Forgiveness

For permissions or inquiries,
contact: mwoolfolkbooks@gmail.com

Printed in the United States of America

ISBN: 979-8-9867579-1-9

For *Her*.
For You.
For Me.
For Us.

Table of Contents

A Word From The Author

As corny as this may sound, this book came to me in a dream.
Or maybe it was *She* who came to me, delivering a message within that dream.
I want to explore the thoughts and feelings that arise
when we speak of the vulva, vagina, and uterus.
Together, they are Etherea.
She is ethereal. *She* is divine.
What do we truly know about *Her*?
What have we forgotten?
I need to—I have to—begin with apologies.
We, as women, have forgotten her, and in doing so, we have forgotten ourselves.
So as we move through these writings, thoughts, and poems,
I ask you to hold *Her*.
Cup *Her* in your hands.
Place your hands upon your pelvis.
Read the apologies aloud, or in your mind.
The ones that resonate—let them become your mantras.
It's time for *Her* to heal.
To be respected.
Adored.
Honored.
Loved.
When *She* heals, we heal.
It is my hope that *She* will be received with an open mind and heart.
That you will allow yourself to feel—without judgment.
That you will find something here that speaks to you.
I hope you enjoy my dream in written form.

Love always,
Mahogany

A Note Before We Begin

Let it be known that the weight of patriarchy has shaped
how women relate to their bodies, their choices,
and their sense of self. It has played a role in how
we have been taught—or not taught—about *She*.

However, this book is not about patriarchy. It is about us.

It is about the emotions we carry, the wounds we inherit,
and the healing we seek. This book is an offering and you
are the altar—a space to reflect, to feel, and to reclaim.

Here, we turn inward.

<u>Prologue</u>

He said he liked me, and that I was pretty.

It was enough for me at the time.

She was willingly given to him in the back of a hyundai,

in a bank parking lot.

Fast, deep thrusts.

She was virgin,

and from his breathing and moans he could not resist.

She received no pleasure.

She received no consideration.

She was just there.

He said I was beautiful, and that I was cool.

Again.

It was enough for me at the time.

She was given willingly to him in her dorm room,

on her bed.

Not virgin,

but he could not resist.

No pleasure

No consideration

She was just there.

I apologize for turning you into an object.

I apologize for being so naive, and careless with you.

I apologize for belittling, and not honoring my womanhood.

How can we be
so detached from
something that is literally
attached to us?
She is the vessel of
creation,
embodying the essence
of strength and femininity.
She is the sacred
gateway.
In her,
lies the
Universe.

Forgive Our Mothers

This chapter is dedicated to forgiving our mothers, and the mothers before us.

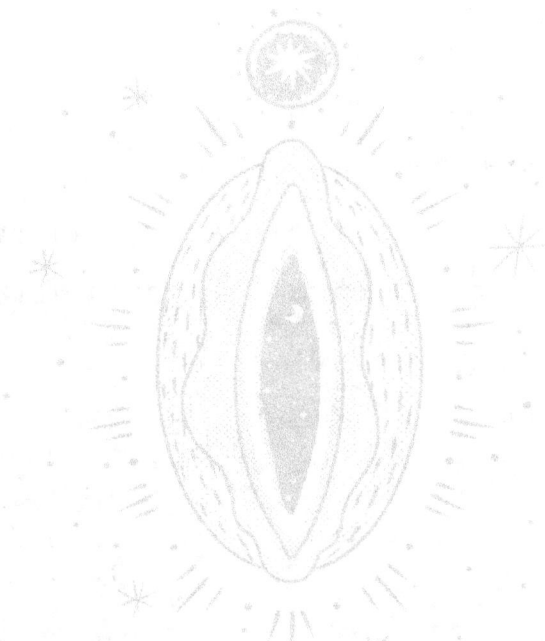

Is *She* not the Mother of all?

How can we fully connect or

deepen our connection with *Her*

if we are uprooted from the mothers

that birthed us?

Taught at an early age that *She* is to be suppressed.

She is for others' pleasure and not our own.

Taught that *Her* blood is "dirty".

Some of us were not told about our cycles,

leaving us scared, and confused.

We have to forgive the timidness within our mothers.

Forgiveness is the first step toward remembering

who *She* truly is.

It is time to unlearn, to remember, to return.

Forgive the mothers before us.
They cannot teach,
What they do not know.

Forgive the mothers
who convinced themselves they did no wrong—or
simply did not know.

Forgive our mothers.
For their hesitant whispers.
For the silences they kept,
In shadows of modesty.
Bound by their own mother's fears.

Forgive the mothers with tightly closed eyes,
ignoring cries in the night.
The mothers with the slippery lovers,
creeping into rooms they should not go.
The mothers who swept their dirt under rugs
just to make themselves comfortable.

Forgive our mothers.
For the lessons left untaught, and words left unsaid.

Forgive the mothers who never told you
you were beautiful.
Leaving you to seek those words
from those with cruel intentions.

Forgive our mothers.
For the gaps in their guidance,
For the truths left unspoken.
For cowering in hesitation,
For lingering in the quiet.

Forgive the mothers who would never be proud of you.
The ones who wished in whispers,
that you were someone else.
Abandoning you to wander.
Losing yourself,
Proving yourself,
Changing yourself.
The mothers who withheld their love
when you needed it most.

Forgive our mothers.
For their fears and uncertainties.
For bonds broken,
For knowledge withheld.

Forgive our mothers.
For the times she did not protect *Her*.
For the moments she was unable to shield *Her* from harm.

Forgive our mothers.

For the moments of disregard.

For her ignorance, and failure to honor *Her* power,

Her sacredness.

Forgive our mothers.
For the veil over truth.
For the love given in fragments.
For carrying wounds that were never theirs.
For passing down what they did not know how to heal.

Forgive the mothers who could not utter the words
"I love you".
Vulnerability was never their strong suit.
They could not speak what they had never
heard or felt.

When we forgive our mothers,
We find our voices.
When we forgive our mothers,
We carve our own paths.
When we forgive our mothers,
We discover our light.
When we forgive our mothers,
She forgives us.

Dandelion Seeds

The children who are never truly gone,
just carried elsewhere.

She was supposed to know.
She was supposed to nourish, to hold,
to bring forth this new soul in the world.
But she didn't.
Did the universe simply change its mind?
Given a seed, *She* was never meant to water.

Tiny footprints carved into the walls of my womb.
Lullabies hummed but never sung.
She remembers, even as my mind whispers
mercy.

They're glowing.
They're blooming.
They're carrying.
I wilt with barren soil in my womb.
Forgive me,
I don't want to feel this.
This penetrative darkness stretching long and coiled
tightly around my neck.

Forgive yourself for feeling as though
Your womb has become a tomb.

How quickly the world moves on,
as I am left behind.
Swallowing it down, again and again,
this bitterness is like an old penny on my tongue.

They speak of God's plan and silver linings.
As if it erases the ache.
As if I should be grateful for a grief
that will not let me go.

Am I wrong to feel that *She*
owes me an explanation?
Was it *Her* choice, or was it fate
that life did not stay?
She is called a sacred place.
A temple of creation.
Yet my creations only whispered their presence,
then slipped into the quiet.

Forgive yourself for the loud thoughts,
for the white lies covered by a seemingly happy smile.
As swollen bellies pass you by,
you hate that their joy feels like theft.

Uninvited green-eyed spirit.
Outwardly you are happy for them,
but inwardly, you only wish you were.

You were planted in my womb,
resting for only a moment.
And like dandelion seeds,
You drifted beyond my reach.
I whispered names into the wind,
watching my ancestors carry you away.
My dandelion seeds, dancing in the wind.
Never truly gone,
just carried elsewhere.

No one tells you how heavy the
nothingness in your womb can be.
How the absence of tiny cries
echo just as loud.
The phantom movements of you
pressed against my ribs.
A life unlived.
Little one, I loved you.
I love you.

Forgive me, little one.
Carrying the weight of what-ifs,
quietly whispering "I love you" in the dark.
You slipped through my fingers like light.

Lay down my sorrow,
Lay down my shame.
My womb is hollow,
I've cried your name.
Am I still worthy?
I don't feel whole.
My soul yearns for mercy,
This is taking its toll.
A gentle prayer,
Softens the pain.
And though I grieve,
I still remain.

Forgive me for not holding on tighter,
for not knowing how to keep you here.
I press my hand where you once were.
Calling out in spaces where no one speaks your name.

She has carried life,
And *She* has lost.
She has celebrated,
And *She* has mourned.
She is dual energy—
Both wound and healer.

You were a flicker.

A star gone before dawn.

My mind wonders, do you blame me

with the same intensity that I blame myself?

Forgive me.

I hope that my love, though brief, was enough.

The little souls cradled in your wombs loved you.
They heard your heartbeat.
They felt your warmth.
These souls, though not meant to stay,
may have been meant to experience your love—
if only for a brief moment.
Forgive yourself for believing you are less of a woman.
You carried life.
No matter how briefly.

Blood at the Roots
Blood in the Seed

This chapter explores the lasting impact of abortion—
on identity, the body, and for
some, even lineage. Blood at the Roots.
It also delves into the sacrifice and emotional weight of
ending a potential life before
it has the chance to grow. Blood in the Seed.

Forgive me,
I have written names in my blood.

The blood remembers.
The choices of my foremothers
are woven into my veins.
Some decisions were let go,
while others, stuck like a fly in a spider's web.

Did they pray?
Did they mourn?
Did they admit their choices aloud in their dreams?
Have we written their fate for them?

And what of me?
Will my past transgression bury itself into my future seed?

I'm not alone in this.
I am one thread woven into this lineage.
Choosing.
Unchoosing.
Carrying.
Releasing.

The blood remembers.

Sing your apologies into the silence.

Unburden yourself in fragments.

One breath,

One tear,

One prayer,

At a time.

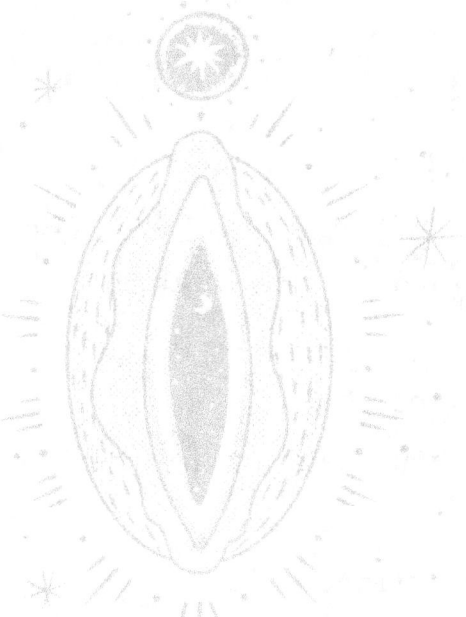

Societal permission.

They call it a "choice".

The right choice for you,

becomes the wrong choice for the many.

Surrounded by scrutiny, fear and regret.

Framed as something personal,

Yet dictated by outside pressures.

What you can,

What you can't,

What's yours?

What's theirs?

I've been marked.
Hester Prynne.
Scarlet Letter "A",
not adultery.
I have been judged,
weighing my womb on Ma'at's scale.
Society is watching.
This is freedom?
Freedom has strings, tangled and frayed.
It's like a contract you sign,
before reading the fine print.

Regret wears many faces.
Forgive me, but the only
regret I feel is not feeling anything.
I don't ask what could've been,
because I never wanted.

Do I need forgiveness?
I chose myself without guilt.
I chose the sunrise, a symbol of a new beginning.
I do not carry weight that is not mine.
I have reclaimed my breath, my body, my future–
without apology.

They wait for my apology.

Forgive me, but that will never come.

I owe no one any tears,

I owe no one sorrow.

They want me to drown in muddy waters of guilt,

when the waters I float in are crystal clear.

They tell me that I will never be whole,

but if I kept the seed, sadly, only then I would be broken.

I can't weep for what was never meant to stay.
No ghosts at my bedside.
I wear no chains of shame around my womb.
No wailing cries in the wind—
only the quiet hum of my own choice.

Regret.

It is not continuous,

But it comes in waves.

Softly on rainy days.

What I could have held,

What I could have nurtured.

It sits in the corners of my room.

Lingers in the crevices of my mind.

An uninvited guest making themselves at home.

Not to haunt, but to remind me of what I could not keep.

Emotional residue.

Unnoticed regret.

I mourn a choice that was not fully mine.

Feelings appearing in unexpected places and times.

In the spaces between laughter, and crying.

A quiet companion along for the journey,

but it doesn't dictate the future.

I reclaim my power over:
My body,
My choices,
My future.
I stand rooted and firm,
breaking the chains of society's pressures.
The only acceptance I need is my own.

I forgive myself.

I stand in the light, as my past sheds off my body,

revealing a new me.

I sit and reflect without judgement.

I allow myself to embrace who I am.

No longer Atlas,

I can take this weight off my shoulders.

I can allow myself to heal knowing that the decision

was made for a reason, no matter the complexities.

I walk forward with a gentle pace,
breathing in the stillness.
With each step, *She* leads me
to the person I am becoming.

From Salted Earth,
Honey Finds the Wound

*Salted earth symbolizes devastation,
conquest, and an attempt to make land barren.
Just as trauma can make the soul feel lifeless,
honey– nature's healer– seeps into even
the deepest wounds. It reminds us that
from pain, sweetness can still emerge.
Healing will find us, in its own time,
in its own way.*

The hands that trespassed against you.

The taking.
　　The tearing.

The silence that screamed after.

You are not the crime.
　　You are not broken.

Most importantly,
You are not the shame
they tried to leave behind.

I'm sorry that they did not see you as

S A C R E D.

Left a gaping wound in your

S P I R I T.

They mistook your softness for

S U R R E N D E R.

You are not what they did.

When the days feel H

       E

        A

         V

          Y,

let the breath that fills your lungs, remind you
that you survived that single moment
that tried to erase you.

State Your Claim

I look around– the faces are all the same.

My body is mine, I announce,
though a chill crawls up my spine.

Laughter erupts, rattling the air.
The gavel slams– a warning, then a glare.

She speaks as if the body was ever hers.
Such a bold statement, what NERVE!
Do you have proof?
A signature?
A witness?

I was born into this body!
That cannot be dismissed!

Irrelevant!
Do you deny men their right to take
what's near?

I deny their right to me!

Gasps.
A hush.
The audacity.
A smirk unfurls on his familiar nightmarish face.

Then tell me.
If your body was truly yours...
Why was it so easy to take?

I weep for the pain *She* endured.

The intrusion into *Her* sacred space.

Scarred by violence,

Shattered by cruelty.

Your essence, violated by force.

She is here with you.

In the silent aftermath, turn to *Her*.

In this sorrow, and trauma etched into your being,

Try to hold and piece together the fragments of your brokenness.

In the depth of this anguish,
I promise to be your guardian.
I apologize for what was beyond my control,
for the nightmare that invaded our peace.
She mourns with you, for the innocence lost,
the trust betrayed, the safety torn away.
Together, we will nurture you with patience and tenderness.
We will honor your resilience, and your strength.

Fear is a Perfume

He follows like a predator.
Scanning for vulnerability like a hunter— cold, calculating.
Power over desire.

She walks with her head down.
I know the ones who fight—
and the ones who freeze.

My mother would not recognize me.

Fear is a perfume,
And I breathe it in.

She looks over her shoulder—
Perfect.

She shouldn't have worn that dress.
She wants us to see.
She's being a tease.

She shouldn't have smiled.
Not like that.
Not at me.

After—
When the sweat cools, and the silence returns,
I stand in front of the mirror.

A man stares back.
Not a monster.

Monsters get caught.

And men like me never do.

A Woman's Rage

I am the match.
The strike.
The wildfire you didn't plan for.
I was reborn from flame.

You thought you could take?
You thought I'd crumble like ash?
Do not mistake my silence for peace.
Hell hath no fury,
I am the storm holding its breath.

I do not scream.
I speak low, and the earth listens.
Tremble before me.
My rage is ancient.
From woman to woman—
each one silenced,
now speaking through me.

Rage has a scent too—
and I wear it like war paint.

Piece by Piece,
breath by breath.
Together we will reclaim our
wholeness.

You are defined by your incredible power to heal.

You rose above the darkness that sought to engulf you.

Every moment, *She* stands with you.

She offers love where there was once pain.

She seeks light where shadows linger.

A story of enduring spirit.
Your scars are a testament to survival.

Stay dedicated to your healing journey.

Restore your peace.

Become a sanctuary of compassion and hope.

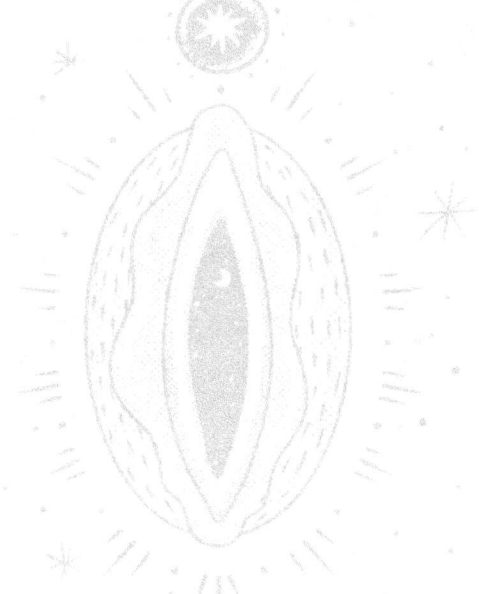

Know that *She* is with you,
unwavering.
In *Her* embrace,
find solace.

If you haven't realized it yet,
I will repeat it again.

You are more than what happened to you.

You are an enduring light.

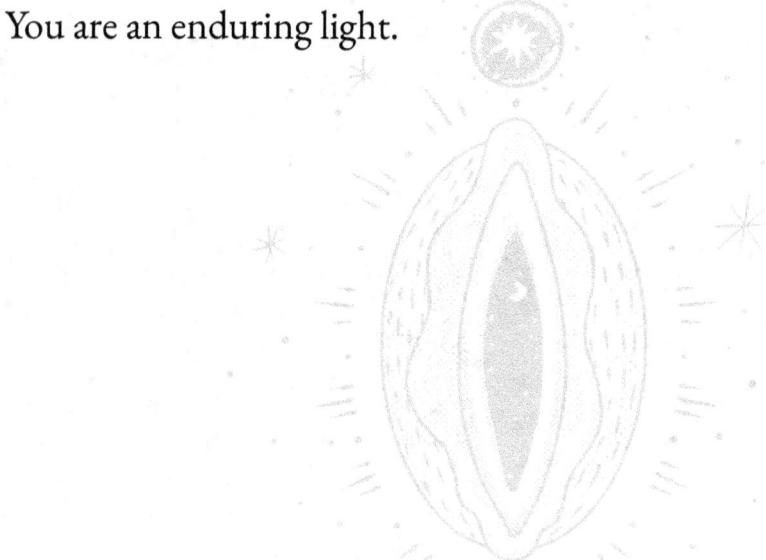

Moist Earth, Wild Roots

This is the chapter of return— of forgiveness and reclamation.
We dig beneath shame and silence.
We unlearn what was taught in fear and relearn what the wild has always known:
Pleasure is not a performance.
It is not one-sided.
She is allowed to bloom.
Let Her roots stretch, Her moisture return.
Let Her become sacred again.

They cannot prey on *Her* and worship *Her*.

Forgive me for letting them
slip their lying tongues inside you
and taste your nectar.

Forgive me for
allowing those with
cold hearts,
sample your warmth.

I'm
  sorry
    for
      allowing
        someone's
        energy
        into
         you,
          thinking
          it
           would
            make
             them
              stay.

I'm
  sorry
    for
      allowing
        someone's
        energy
        into
         you,
          because
          I
           thought
           it
            was
             love.

I'm
sorry
for
allowing
someone's
energy
into
you,
because
I
didn't
love
myself.

I'm
sorry
for
giving
you
to
someone
who
never
knew
how
to
appreciate
you.

I apologize
for not
exploring and
knowing you
first, before
letting another
do so.

Forgive yourself for the shame you carried,
in moments of self discovery.

 In learning to please yourself,
in exploring your desires, you reclaimed your power.

No more hesitation, no more fear.
Your pleasure is not a sin.

Our disappointed sighs have become the clouds in the sky.
Heavy with rain– like the tears we hold back.

The great pretenders.
How many times have we lied to keep the peace?
Or to make our partners feel better?

How many times have we left *Her* frustrated?
Smiling through it all, receiving no satisfaction.

Giving you a pat on the back, clapping for you like a trained seal.
My soul stayed silent, as *She* filled with rage with every fake applause.

Unspoken desires suppressed.
Longing for *Her* needs to be met,
while prioritizing others instead.
Her pleasure became an afterthought.
She learned to starve in silence.

She Is Not Them

He touches me like a script.
Like I'm supposed to moan on cue.

Oh, you've studied the female body?
You have your degree in "how to please _Her_"?
A degree you earned from your exes?

Fascinating.

Lover, your confidence is adorable—
But let me let you in on something...

You missed the way I held back,
The way my hips gyrated to guide you gently.
The way my eyes closed— not from pleasure,
but from wishing I was elsewhere.

I wonder, how many fake orgasms
you've added to your resume
like they were real victories.

Your name will never echo between these thighs
If you refuse to learn _Her_ language.

Same Parts, Still Lost

"We're the same," she whispered,
as if our shared anatomy
granted her mastery.
She came to me with such certainty,
and lips full of promise.

She thought knowing her body
meant she knew mine.
She didn't ask.
Didn't watch how I tensed.
Didn't listen for the breath I held.

I am not a mirror.
I am a terrain she never studied.
A language she assumed she spoke.

How can pleasure be silent?
How can I love what I feel
without giving it a voice?

This body is mine,
and it will speak every moan,
and every sigh,
without apology.

I have been taught
to keep my voice soft,
to keep my rapture hidden,
as if it's wrong to be loud with what feels good.

I am not ashamed of my euphoric cry,
that reverberates through the air
and shakes the ground beneath us.

No more hushed pleasure.
No more holding back.
She will take what is hers
and make sure you hear it.

I want.

My desire is not dirty.

She aches.

She craves.

No sin in the way my body

responds to the thought of being

touched.

She is awakened.

And *She* will not hide.

She is not one-size-fits-all.

Her pleasure shifts like the tides.

She is not a conquest,

She is a conversation.

To love *Her* is to ask, not assume.

To please *Her* is to listen, not ignore.

And after all the unlearning,
the reclaiming,
the passionate moans once silenced,
and the shame unburdened.
She returns.
Not just to pleasure,
but to power.
To the sacred memory
of who she's always been.

When *She* remembers who *She* is,
even the stars
pause and stare.

She:

Forgiveness

Acknowledgments

To my husband, Ricardo.

Your love and unwavering support have kept me grounded on this journey.
Thank you for always being my anchor, my earth sign that keeps this water sign in touch u
reality when I need it most.
You believed in me even when I couldn't believe in myself.
I love you.

To my daughters, Narra & Remedy.
You both inspire me everyday with your boundless love, freedom of self, and strength.
You are the future I write for.
I love you.

To the women in my life *who read,*
critiqued, and held space for me as I birthed this book.
Your honesty and encouragement gave me the courage to keep going,
to dig deeper, and to stay true to my voice without fear.

To all women— *this is for you.*
Your stories, your struggles, your tears, your pleasures, and your reclamation.
You are sacred.

Acknowledgments

To my ancestors.
Your wisdom flows through my veins, and your spirits guided my hands as I wrote.
I stand on your shoulders.

To She, who came to me in a dream.
You awakened a power in me that I can no longer ignore.
Thank you for guiding me to this truth, for sparking the fire of this book within me,
and for showing me the power of my own voice.
You are the inspiration behind every word and the heartbeat of this work.

And to myself—
Thank you for the courage to share my truth- and the truths of others.
Thank you for creating something that was always within me.
This book is as much a gift to myself as it is to the world.

Final Note From The Author

Writing this book has been a journey of bravery—
of embracing the raw, the beautiful, and the unapologetic.
Each poem is a reflection of my truth, but also the truths of countless
others who have been afraid to speak their own. Through these pages,
I hope to give a voice to those who have been silenced,
to illuminate the beauty in our pleasure, and to honor the sacredness of
every woman's body and experience.

My hope is that this book serves as both an invitation and a reminder—
to awaken to our desires without shame, to embrace our power
without fear, and to honor our bodies as the sacred temples they are.

To anyone who reads this, I invite you to walk boldly on this path
of self-love, of speaking your truth, and of celebrating the divine force
that lives within you.

About the Author

Mahogany is a passionate writer, poet,
and creator who believes in the power of self-expression and the importance of
reclaiming one's voice. With a deep love for exploring themes of femininity, desire,
pleasure, and healing, Mahogany channels
personal experiences and the stories of
others into words that speak to the
heart and soul.

Mahogany's work invites readers to
embrace the beauty in their own
vulnerability and strength, encouraging
them to step into their power
unapologetically. When not writing,
Mahogany is a loving mother, wife,
and student, constantly seeking balance
in both the creative and practical aspects
of life.

Her work is deeply inspired by her own
journey of self-discovery and the women
who have shaped her path. This book is a
testament to the power of reclaiming
one's truth and standing firmly in the
light of who we are.

Invitation to Connect

I would love to hear from you!
Whether you've been inspired by the words within these pages
or have a thought to share, I invite you to connect with me.

Join me in creating a space for self-love, healing, and unapologetic truth.

Follow me on social media:

Instagram: @mwoolfolkbooks

Tiktok: tiktok.com/@mwoolfolkbooks

Threads: @mwoolfolkbooks

Twitter/X: @mwoolfolkbooks

Facebook: Mahogany Desiree

Website: www.mahoganywoolfolkbooks.com

For inquiries, collaborations, or just to share your journey, feel free to reach out a
Email: mwoolfolkbooks@gmail.com

Thank you for being part of this conversation.

www.ingramcontent.com/pod-product-compliance
Lightning Source LLC
Chambersburg PA
CBHW070348130626
46556CB00007B/3082